I0813545

Singing Justice Singing Peace

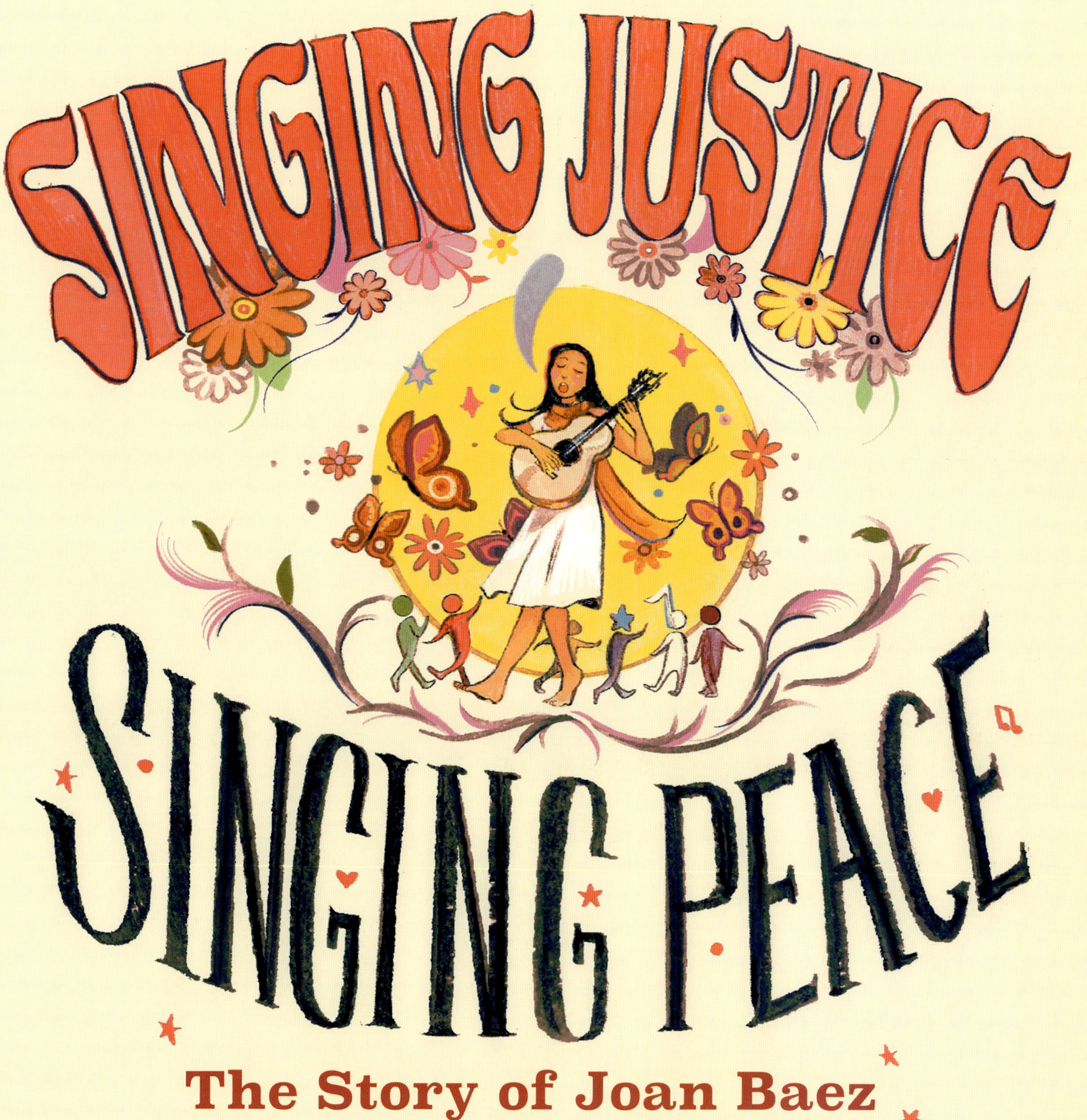

The Story of Joan Baez

Written by Monica Brown
Illustrated by Molly Mendoza

Beach Lane Books New York Amsterdam/Antwerp London Toronto Sydney/Melbourne New Delhi

As a little girl, Joan Baez loved to be the center of attention—dancing, acting, making jokes, and especially singing! Her beautiful and gentle voice was a gift.

Joan was the daughter of immigrants from Mexico and Scotland. Joan's parents taught her that she was born of many nations and that all humans are brothers and sisters.

Joan loved her family very much.

But Joan *didn't* always love going to school. She preferred staying home with her mom and exploring outside—running barefoot, climbing trees, collecting insects, picking flowers, and building little cities out of sand and sticks.

Joan's father was a scientist, and when his company wanted him to work on weapons, he refused and quit. He believed he could use science, creativity, and compassion to change the world and make it a better place.

By the time Joan was five, she knew she wanted to make the world a better place too.

Someday she would.

Joan's father joined a peace organization that sent the Baez family to Iraq.

Joan soon learned that not all children had enough to eat and that many went to bed hungry each night. Some parents even had to search through other people's trash to find food for their families. The more Joan learned about the poor around the world and in the United States, the more she worried.

"Don't carry the whole world on your shoulders," Joan's mother said.

To make herself feel better, Joan sang, and those who heard her beautiful voice felt better too.

A REPUBLIC

When Joan's family moved back to California, Joan didn't feel like she belonged. Some kids called her names because she was Mexican, while others said she wasn't Mexican enough because she didn't speak Spanish. Joan just wanted to be herself.

Joan's parents gave her a ukulele, and it changed her life forever. When Joan plucked on the strings and sang, she found her power.

Now Joan sang all the time, even in math class, where she got in trouble!

Joan soon traded in her ukulele for a guitar and began learning songs by Della Reese, Eartha Kitt, Harry Belafonte, and Odetta Holmes. Odetta was known as "the Queen of Folk," a type of music by the people and for the people, passed down across generations. From Odetta, Joan learned to sing "Oh, Freedom!," a song about liberty.

Joan loved to sing barefoot, with her feet kissing the earth.

Joan was only sixteen when she first heard singer Pete Seeger perform "If I Had a Hammer," a song about justice and equality for workers. Joan dreamed of inspiring others with music as Pete did.

One day a young Dr. Martin Luther King Jr. came to speak at Joan's high school. He said that hate must be fought with weapons of love. From Dr. King, Joan learned of the bus boycotts and the struggle for equality and freedom. She learned about nonviolence, which she believed was organized love.

She was inspired.

Joan realized music could move people's hearts, minds, and feet toward a path of justice and peace. She decided to use the gift of her voice to do just that.

CLUB 47

After high school, Joan moved to Boston, where she sang in coffee shops and clubs. She sang songs about workers, civil rights, and the struggle for justice. People started to know her name and her voice.

Then Joan was invited to Chicago, where the great singer Odetta asked her to perform. It was Joan's first folk festival, and she was scared to step out onstage, but with her guitar in hand, she decided that if she shook, she would shake with courage.

Wearing her bright orange rebozo, Joan sang in her bare feet. The audience loved her! They didn't want her to stop singing, and they chanted, "More, more, more!"

Joan began singing at folk music festivals all over the country, and her words flew into people's hearts. She recorded her first album—barefoot, of course!

Joan joined the struggle for justice, singing to encourage the marchers in the Civil Rights Movement, led by Dr. King and other brave people.

In New York City, Joan met a musician named Bob Dylan. When Joan sang Bob's amazing lyrics with her incredible voice, the people listened! Joan invited Bob up onstage to sing beside her at the Newport Folk Festival, and together they sang for peace. They became known across the world.

Joan's voice was beautiful and gentle, her message fierce and strong!

Then, on August 28, 1963, came Joan's most important performance yet. In front of the Lincoln Memorial in Washington, DC, twenty-two-year-old Joan Baez stood next to her hero, Dr. Martin Luther King Jr., at the March on Washington. Joan sang "We Shall Overcome" and "Oh, Freedom!" to hundreds of thousands of marchers.

Soon it was time for Reverend King to take the stage and share his dream of justice, equality, and freedom for all people, regardless of the color of their skin.

After the March on Washington, Joan kept singing songs of justice, songs of peace.

In 1965, Joan sang as she marched from Selma to Montgomery in support of the Civil Rights Movement.

She sang Bob Dylan's "The Times They Are A-Changin'" in protest of the Vietnam War.

She looked into the eyes of President Lyndon B. Johnson and asked him to listen to the voices of young people who wanted peace, not war.

No nos moverán
¡Sí se puede!
Asimbonanga

She sang with César Chávez and Dolores Huerta in support of farmworkers.

She sang against apartheid in South Africa.

Joan's amazing voice reached millions of people around the world—in the Americas, Africa, Asia, and Europe.

Joan sang with love, and her words rose high in the sky like stars, giving listeners the courage and light to fight for justice.

Joan Baez, the barefoot teenager with a guitar, grew up to sing for presidents and other leaders, but mostly for the everyday people she loved—the people willing to fight for equality and fairness.

When Joan Baez was inducted into the Rock & Roll Hall of Fame, she said, “Together let us build a bridge, a great bridge, a beautiful bridge to once again welcome the tired and the poor.”

Joan Baez still believes that each of us can create change.

And still she sings songs of justice, songs of peace.

Author's Note

It is my hope that readers will come to this book inspired by Joan Baez's music, and finish reading it inspired by her commitment to making our world a more peaceful, just place.

Joan is a singer, songwriter, artist, and peace activist. All her life, Joan has used her incredible voice in the service of social justice, pacifism, and civil rights for everyone. Though Joan released dozens of records—including eight gold albums—and won countless prestigious awards, including a Grammy Lifetime Achievement Award, I did not write about her solely because of her musical talent. Rather, what astounded me during my research was the way she has boldly and consistently used her musical gifts to stand up for the basic human rights of others. Joan's profound commitment to nonviolent action in support of social justice resounds today.

Joan committed her first act of civil disobedience as a teenager in high school, by refusing to participate in an air raid drill. She was influenced greatly by her Quaker parents: her father, Albert Baez, a scientist and Mexican immigrant who refused to work on nuclear weapons, and her mother, Joan Chandos Bridge, a Scottish immigrant who once went to jail with her daughter for protesting the draft during the Vietnam War. As a teenager, Joan saw Pete Seeger, a leading folk singer, in concert, and she realized the power of music to move people. Activist Ira Sandperl, an early mentor, introduced Joan at a young age to thinkers like Gandhi and Thoreau. But perhaps her greatest influence was Dr. Martin Luther King Jr.

She first heard Dr. King speak in 1956, the same year she bought her first guitar. His example would inspire her the rest of her life. She was already a famous folk singer in 1963, when she stood in front of the Lincoln Memorial in Washington, DC, and sang to the hundreds of thousands gathered for the March on Washington. Joan then watched Dr. King as he set aside his prepared speech and breathed the power of thunder into his words. There were many times she used her voice in support of the Civil Rights Movement. Once, when she was in Mississippi to support school integration, she was called upon to help wake Dr. King from a nap. Tired from his endless work, he was fast asleep, and Joan sat in a chair near his bed and sang softly and then more and more loudly the lyrics to "Oh, Freedom!"

Joan's songs helped mobilize an anti-war movement in protest of the Vietnam War. She believed pacifism was more important than required military service. When she sang Bob Dylan's "Blowin' in the Wind," she told the audience to be strong in their convictions and to use love to seek change.

Even as Joan found fame and success as a musician, her commitment to peace and social change never wavered. She founded the Institute for the Study of Nonviolence, which grew into the Resource Center for Nonviolence (rcnv.org), and she worked to found the first Amnesty International office in the United States. Joan sang to workers and mothers across South America, she sang against South Africa's apartheid, she sang to those hurting in Sarajevo, and she sang to President Barack Obama at his first presidential inauguration. Always, her voice brought hope and healing.

Joan Baez knows that the work of making the world a better place is never finished. May she inspire all of us to lift our voices in support of a more just and peaceful world.

Sources

Baez, Joan. *And a Voice to Sing With: A Memoir.* New York: Simon & Schuster, 2009.

Baez, Joan. *Daybreak*. New York: Dial Press, 1968.

Hajdu, David. *Positively 4th Street: The Lives and Times of Joan Baez, Bob Dylan, Mimi Baez Fariña, and Richard Fariña*. New York: Farrar, Straus and Giroux, 2011.

Joan Baez. "Bio Info." Accessed July 21, 2020. http://www.joanbaez.com/bio/.

King, Martin Luther, Jr. "I Have A Dream." https://www.naacp.org/i-have-a-dream-speech-full-march-on-washington/.

Rock & Roll Hall of Fame. "Joan Baez." https://www.rockhall.com/inductees/joan-baez.

Wharton, Mary, dir. *Joan Baez: How Sweet the Sound*. WNET, 2009.

For Theo, I sing to you with love
—M. B.

To my dad and his guitar
—M. M.

BEACH LANE BOOKS
An imprint of Simon & Schuster Children's Publishing Division
1230 Avenue of the Americas, New York, New York 10020

Book design by Sonia Chaghatzbanian

The text for this book was set in Superclarendon.
The illustrations for this book were drawn in Sumi ink on mixed media paper and colored digitally using Procreate.
Manufactured in China
Manf code 1025 SCP
First Edition
2 4 6 8 10 9 7 5 3 1
Names: Brown, Monica, 1969- author. | Mendoza, Molly, illustrator.
Title: Singing justice, singing peace : the story of Joan Baez / Monica Brown ; illustrated by Molly Mendoza.
Description: New York : Beach Lane Books, 2026. | Audience: Ages 4–8 | Audience: Grades 2–3 | Summary: "An illuminating picture book biography of renowned Mexican-American folk musician Joan Baez, whose songs of justice, peace, and activism have inspired listeners to create positive change across the world"—Provided by publisher.
Identifiers: LCCN 2025004807 (print) | LCCN 2025004808 (ebook) | ISBN 9781665926607 (hardcover) | ISBN 9781665926614 (ebook)
Subjects: LCSH: Baez, Joan—Juvenile literature. | Singers—United States—Biography—Juvenile literature. | Mexican Americans—Biography—Juvenile literature. | Political activists—United States—Biography—Juvenile literature. | Pacifists—United States—Biography—Juvenile literature.
Classification: LCC ML3930.B205 B76 2026 (print) | LCC ML3930.B205 (ebook) | DDC 782.42162/130092 [B]—dc23/eng/20250211
LC record available at https://lccn.loc.gov/2025004807
LC ebook record available at https://lccn.loc.gov/2025004808